D1326789

FOOD & FEASTS

in
Tudor Times

Richard Balkwill

LIBRARY
CHARLESTON ACADEMY
INVERNESS

Wayland

FOOD & FEASTS

Titles in the series

In Ancient Egypt
In Ancient Greece
In Ancient Rome
With the Vikings
In the Middle Ages
With the Aztecs
In Tudor Times
Between the Two World Wars

A ZOË BOOK

© 1995 Zoë Books Limited

Devised and produced by
Zoë Books Limited
15 Worthy Lane
Winchester
Hampshire SO23 7AB
England

Apart from any fair dealing for the purposes of research or private study, or criticism or review, as permitted under the Copyright, Designs and Patents Act, 1988, this publication may only be reproduced, stored or transmitted, in any form or by any means, with the prior permission in writing of the publishers, or in the case of reprographic reproduction in accordance with the terms of licences issued by the Copyright Licensing Agency.

Any person who does any unauthorised act in relation to this publication may be liable to criminal prosecution and civil claims for damages.

First published in Great Britain in 1995 by
Wayland (Publishers) Ltd
61 Western Road, Hove
East Sussex BN3 1JD

British Library Cataloguing in Publication Data

Balkwill, Richard
  Food and Feasts in Tudor Times
  I. Title
  394.1209409031

ISBN 0-7502-1131-8

Printed in Italy by Grafedit SpA.
Design: Jan Sterling, Sterling Associates
Picture Research: Victoria Sturgess
Map: Gecko Limited
Production: Grahame Griffiths

Photographic acknowledgments

The publishers wish to acknowledge, with thanks, the following photographic sources:

Ancient Art & Architecture Collection 3,25r; Bibliothèque Nationale, Paris 11b,23b; The Bridgeman Art Library 5b,11t / British Library 6 / British Museum 24 / Giraudon title page / Kunsthistorisches Museum, Vienna 12,17 / Phillips 14; The British Library, London 16b,19,21t; Mary Evans Picture Library 5t,8r,9b,21b,22; The Feathers Hotel, Ludlow 23t; Glasgow Museums, The Burrell Collection 8l; Department of Printing & Graphic Arts, The Houghton Library, Harvard University 10,13b; Louvre, Paris © photo R.M.N. 9r; courtesy of The Marquess of Salisbury 18; courtesy of Museum of Fine Arts, Boston 7bl&r,16t; National Gallery of Scotland 25l; Roger-Viollet / Boyer 13t; The Royal Collection © 1994 Her Majesty Queen Elizabeth II 15t,20; The Board of the Trustees of the Victoria & Albert Museum 15b; The Warburg Institute, University of London 7t.

Cover: The Bridgeman Art Library / British Library centre / Giraudon bottom; Mary Evans Picture Library top left & right

The publishers have made every effort to trace the copyright holders, but if they have inadvertently overlooked any, they will be pleased to make the necessary arrangement at the first opportunity.

04497
942.05

Contents

Introduction

Welshman called Owen Tudor, who died in 1461, gave the Tudor period its name. His grandson, Henry Tudor, founded the Tudor ruling family, or **dynasty**, which lasted from 1485 until 1603. Henry became King Henry VII in 1485, after winning the Battle of Bosworth. Other Tudor **monarchs** were Henry VIII, Edward VI, Mary, and Elizabeth I.

The kings and queens of England at this time ruled a country with a tiny, scattered population. There were fewer than 5 million people, compared with today's 56 million. Towns were small. None in England or Wales had a population of more than 200,000. Venice and Paris were bigger than London.

In Europe and in the rest of the world, great changes took place during the hundred years from 1500 to 1600. Explorers travelled by sea to parts of the world not known to many Europeans. Christopher Columbus landed in what is now America in 1492, while Vasco da Gama reached India. In 1522, Magellan became the first person to sail around the world.

Sir Francis Drake also sailed around the world. In 1577 he returned to England with gold and silver from the Caribbean

Kings and Queens of England

Henry VII 1485-1509
Henry VIII 1509-1547
Edward VI 1547-1553
Mary I 1553-1558
Elizabeth I 1558-1603

Kings of France

Charles VIII 1483-1498
Louis XII 1498-1515
François I 1515-1547
Henri II 1547-1559
François II 1559-1560
Charles IX 1560-1574
Henri III 1574-1589
Henri IV 1589-1610

Holy Roman Empire

Charles V 1519-1556

Spain

Philip II 1556-1598

▽ The main voyages of discovery and Europe in Tudor Times

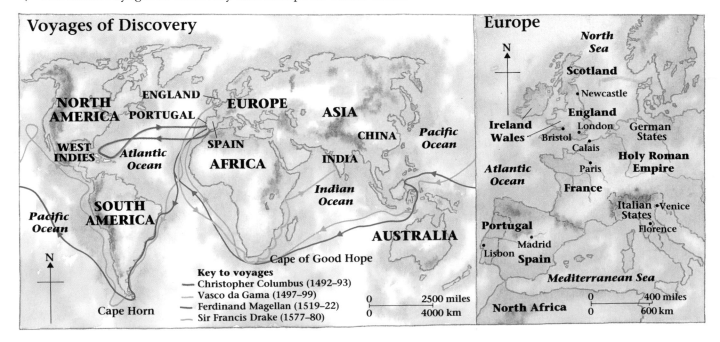

Voyages of Discovery

NORTH AMERICA
WEST INDIES
Atlantic Ocean
SOUTH AMERICA
Pacific Ocean
ENGLAND
PORTUGAL
EUROPE
SPAIN
AFRICA
ASIA
CHINA
INDIA
Pacific Ocean
Indian Ocean
AUSTRALIA
Cape of Good Hope
Cape Horn
N

Key to voyages
— Christopher Columbus (1492–93)
— Vasco da Gama (1497–99)
— Ferdinand Magellan (1519–22)
— Sir Francis Drake (1577–80)

0   2500 miles
0   4000 km

Europe

North Sea
Scotland
• Newcastle
England
Ireland • London German States
Wales • Bristol
• Calais
Atlantic Ocean
• Paris
France
Holy Roman Empire
Italian States • Venice
Portugal
• Madrid • Florence
• Lisbon Spain
Mediterranean Sea
North Africa
N

0   400 miles
0   600 km

△ This woodcut shows an Italian kitchen. It is from a cookery book by Christoforo di Messisburgo, published in Ferrara, Italy, in 1549.

Dough is being rolled out on the left. Two assistants are turning the **spits**. A rather tiny man is fanning the fire with a pair of bellows. Joints of meat and birds have been prepared. The dog has a bone to chew.

One of the earliest printed recipe books was written in French by an Italian, Lancelot de Casteau. It was called *Ouverture de Cuisine*, and was published in Liège, Belgium in 1604.

and Mexico, as well as spices such as ginger and pepper. Sir Walter Raleigh brought new foods, such as maize (or corn) and potatoes, from the New World. He also introduced tobacco, which was thought to be a cure for illness.

Travel by land was slow and difficult. But in Europe, wealth and knowledge were increasing. In Italy, people began to be interested in the arts and sciences of ancient Greece and Rome. They studied the medicine, mathematics, literature, sculpture and buildings of the ancient world. This movement, known as the **Renaissance** (or 'rebirth'), spread across Europe.

The invention of the printing press made it easier for ideas and information to be exchanged. People were able to read about what happened in other countries, as well as about the ways of life, or lifestyles, of different peoples. It was possible to read about food in other parts of the world, too, from the recipe books which were printed at about this time.

▽ 'Summer' by Arcimboldo, 1563. This painting seems to be a picture of freshly picked summer fruit and vegetables. But look more closely and you will also see a man sitting and looking up to the left. His hair is made up of grapes, his cheeks are mushrooms, his arms are celery and his legs and feet are maize and turnips.

Farming and food in the countryside

The kind of food eaten by people in Tudor times depended on the type of family into which a person was born. There were huge differences between the lives of rich and poor people. Rich people ate a wide variety of food, including plenty of meat and fish. Feasts or **banquets** were often held at the ruler's court. Meanwhile, in the countryside, poor people ate whatever they could grow or raise, on land which did not belong to them, in a climate that was often wet and cold.

The summers of 1594, 1595, 1596 and 1597 were cold and wet. Crops could not be harvested, and they rotted in the fields. This led to food shortages, or **famine**, and riots.

Life on the land

For hundreds of years, people in the country-side had lived under the **feudal** system. The land owner, who lived in a castle or **manor** house,

▷ This illustration of 'Ploughing, sowing and harrowing' comes from an English book made in 1520.

In the background two horses are pulling a plough. The man with a whip is driving a horse-drawn **harrow**, used to break up and flatten the earth. Someone else is sowing seeds by scattering, or **broadcasting**, them. All these things would not happen at the same time; the painter is trying to show the details together in the same picture.

▷ This country scene was engraved by Jacob Matham in 1603. It was based on a picture by the Dutch painter Pieter Aertens. There are baskets of fresh fruit and vegetables, and there are eggs and a cockerel or chicken. In the background, farm workers are resting.

controlled all the land in an area. People worked in the owner's fields, and also on small pieces of land where they grew food for their own families. Cattle, sheep and horses were owned by wealthy people, while the poor tenants might keep a pig or two. Poor people were allowed to graze their animals on common land.

This system was slowly changing in England and Wales in Tudor times. In some areas, land owners began to keep more sheep, and to grow fewer crops. Instead of working on the owner's land, the tenants paid rent for their small plots.

▽ These pictures are from *The Twelve Months*, by Virgil Solis. They show winter work in the countryside. In 'November,' pigs are fattened on acorns and cattle are killed.

▽ In 'December', pigs are killed and the meat is prepared for cooking. The hams are being put to soak in salted water, or **brine**.

William Harrison wrote in his *Description of England*, published in 1577, that when times were hard, people had to content themselves with, 'bread made of beans, peas or oats, or all together, and some acorns too.'

The changes brought problems when some open fields were fenced in, or **enclosed**, and poorer people had nowhere to grow food.

Food for land workers

The most important food for country people was a thick soup, or **pottage**. It was made with vegetables such as cabbage and broad beans, and was thickened with oatmeal or barley. Sometimes meat might be added. Root vegetables such as turnips and swedes were grown, but potatoes were not known until later in the Tudor period. People ate salads made of onions, radishes, garlic and cucumber, as well as lettuce. Tomatoes were also unknown.

Most villages had their own baker. The oven was heated and mounds of dough were put into it. Then the oven door was sealed up with mud. A skilled baker knew exactly when to break open the door and remove the cooked bread.

Bread was usually made into buns, rather than loaves. The best quality bread was called *manchet*, and the less good was called *cheat*. People still used a flat wedge of bread, or *trencher* as a mat or plate. Juices from the food they ate would soak into the bread. Sometimes the used *trenchers* were given to poor people.

For the worker in the country, meat was a rare treat on feast days. An ox, a sheep or a pig might be roasted by turning it on a spike, or spit, over an open fire. Pork from pigs was usually salted, or smoked to make ham and bacon. It was **preserved** in this way to

▽ These pictures of 'The Bakers of York' were drawn in 1595. You can see a couple checking grain or flour, another person kneading dough, followed by the baking and selling of the bread. The words over the top encourage the baker to do his job well!

▽ This 16th century German picture shows a wild boar being killed for the kitchen, while someone else is chopping down a tree. It is hard to tell why the man on the right has been put in the **stocks**.

Populations around 1500

England and Wales: 4.5 million people (12 million sheep)

London: 75,000

Venice: 180,000

Paris: 240,000

prevent it from going bad. Meat such as mutton from sheep and venison from deer was eaten by richer people.

No one was allowed to eat meat on Fridays. On this day, people ate fish. It usually came from freshwater rivers and ponds. Carp, pike, eels and trout were eaten. Sea food would go bad before it reached the table, unless you lived near the sea.

Anything that flew was considered suitable food, especially pigeons. Birds which we would now protect from harm such as bittern, storks and larks, were also killed and eaten. Dovecotes were built in the gardens of large houses as a larder. The birds would gather there, build nests and breed, providing a source of food, particularly in very cold winters.

Fruit such as strawberries and cherries grew for a short time in the summer and did not keep. Apples and pears were more common, as well as a type of cooking apple known as a *pomewater*. In the early 1600s, travellers from Spain and North Africa began to bring back oranges and lemons, but they did not often reach people in the country. The climate in England was usually not hot enough to grow grapes, apricots and peaches, though these were common in Europe. Figs, dates and raisins were **imported** luxuries.

What did people drink at this time? The dried leaf which is used to make tea and the roasted bean which makes coffee were still unknown in Europe. Instead, **ale**, which tasted like weak beer, was the usual drink, for adults and children alike. Cider from apples, perry

▽ A woodcut made in 1510 shows a cook removing the insides from, or gutting, a hare. Pots are cooking on and over the fire, and ladles are hanging on the wall.

△ This 16th century enamelled dish shows a well-tended garden, full of a rich variety of fruits. Pomona, 'the fair gardener' seems to be supervising the work, rather than doing it herself.

Sully, a minister at
the court of Henri IV
of France, wrote:
'Tilling the land
and tending the
flocks are the two
breasts from which
France is fed.'

from pears, and mead from honey were also drunk. Wine was the drink at court and for the nobles and rich people. It was brought to Britain, or imported, from France and Spain, but it was often so nasty that water or sugar was usually added.

People in the country did not eat breakfast. They usually ate two meals a day. Dinner was served at 11, and supper at 4 o'clock. In summer, haymakers and harvesters would take bread and an onion, with an apple, cake or pasty, into the fields, together with ale or cider. In hard winters there was very little food, and there would be nothing fresh to eat. Poor people lived on thin soup, or **broth**, and dried peas.

A gentleman's life

A gentleman who lived in Normandy, France, kept a journal of his life in the country from 1549 to 1563. He was called Gilles de Gouberville, and he gives a very good picture of what it was like to live a comfortable life. He grew apples and pears in his orchard, and made cider and perry, as well as a strong drink we now call *Calvados*. He kept bees, and a man would come to collect the honey, often also killing an animal for meat during his visit.

Gilles de Gouberville lived near the sea at Cherbourg so he often ate fresh fish. He also

An important book of the time gave information on farming, and the cultivation of vegetables. It was called *Theatre de l'agriculture*, written by Olivier de Serres, and was first published in Paris in 1600. It contains many engravings showing the best way of growing things successfully. In one picture you can see the master and mistress surveying their home. In the background, a gardener is pushing a wheelbarrow, and a workman is **threshing** corn. A dairymaid churns butter in her dairy, while hens, chickens and pigs scavenge for food in the yard.

▽ This scene of French country house life, from *Theatre de l'agriculture*, is by Olivier de Serres. You can see that food for the house came from the dovecote, the fishpond, the beehives and the poultry yard.

ate cabbage, broad beans, turnips, beetroot, peas, spinach and lettuce. For meat, he had plenty of veal (calf-meat), **offal** and black pudding. He also ate storks, eels and carp. The journal describes him sitting in his kitchen (where the animals were killed and cut up into joints of meat), doing his accounts and dozing in front of the fire.

△ This painting is called 'A man and a woman before a table laid with fruit and vegetables'. You can see peas and chestnuts, as well as apples, pears and cherries.

▷ This 16th century picture shows olive oil being made. The olives are being poured into a vat (left) and then ground by a big stone. The oil is collected in jars, or carried away in barrels.

Food in towns and cities

Life in towns and cities for most people in Tudor times was dirty and noisy. Disease was common. Rubbish and human waste, **sewage**, were dumped straight into the rivers. In London, there was a filthy stream which flowed into the River Thames, called the Fleet Ditch. People had no idea that there was any link between illness and keeping clean.

Most Tudor towns were very small compared with today's towns. In London, the area known as Chelsea was a market garden deep in the country. Houses in towns had their own 'back-side', a small plot of garden or yard, in which to grow vegetables or keep a pig. In Manchester, pigs hunted through rubbish in the streets for food. Many people ate a simple and probably boring diet of boiled beef pottage, bread and ale.

Staying in towns

Towns were the centres of trade and wealth. Traders and **merchants** bought and sold, and

▽ This 16th century Dutch painting is by Lucas van Valkenbosch. It shows a lady with her children shopping for vegetables. You can see cabbages, cauliflowers, beans and a cucumber. The red fruits in the baskets are cherries. In the background there is the marketplace where people are looking at and buying fresh produce.

Henry VIII was a huge man who liked to eat well. In big cities, he and other members of his court would often carry a piece of orange when they were out among the people. The king would hold the orange piece under his nose in order to mask the foul smells of towns and unwashed people.

△ Monks making wine at Saint-Germain-des-Prés in Paris.

Many vineyards were destroyed in times of war. When the monks started to grow vines again, they hid the wine in cellars. The cold dark conditions turned out to be ideal for storing the wine.

The dangers of gluttony

Olivier de Serres wrote in 1600: 'When a gentleman attains an income of £500, he no longer knows what it is to eat well, because, wishing to eat in the grand style, he eats in the *salle* (dining room) at the mercy of his cook, where previously he had taken his meals in the kitchen, having himself served according to his own tastes.'

more and more goods were sent to other countries in exchange for gold and silver, herbs and spices, and new kinds of food.

In towns and cities, inns and **taverns** served a wide range of food to merchants and travellers. Drinking was often on a grand scale, and so was the drunkenness which followed it! Beer, ale, cider and wine were served, including *clairet*, a light clear red wine which is now called claret. Darker, thicker red wines came from Spain, as well as port wine from Portugal.

In schools and hospitals, as well as universities and inns of court (where lawyers were trained), dinner was served at 12 noon and supper at 5 o'clock. Meals were expensive for visitors, but pupils and students could afford to eat quite well. Fruit, milk, vegetables, eggs and salad, with meat or fish served once a day, gave them a good diet. People who could not make a living because they were old, poor or sick, went to live in the poorhouse. Poorhouse food was plain and simple: rye bread, porridge, cheese, salted herrings, and beer.

Rich people could afford to eat plenty of meat. A country squire named William Darrell came to London from Wiltshire, and was 'detained by matters of law'. He took rooms, and ate well. Joints of beef and mutton were served, along with side dishes of **game** (including rabbits, pigeons and pheasants). He was served bread, butter and cheese, with beer to drink. The main vegetables he ate were dried peas, which suggests it was winter. On Friday, he noted that he was served carp, pike and salted herring.

Town kitchens

We get a clear idea from pictures and journals of the time of how people ate in towns. Most kitchens did not have what

▽ This woodcut shows a bakeshop. Bread and pies are being cooked. Logs of wood are drying on the rack above the oven.

◁ This kitchen scene shows a mass of fascinating detail. The artist, Floris van Schooten, has painted items of cooking equipment, as well as a full range of fruits, including pomegranates, melons and gooseberries, and vegetables such as artichokes. There are also joints of pork, smoked fish, sausages, cheese and larks. The people at the table may be eating or playing a game. Perhaps one of them has come to sell produce to the others.

we would call a cooker. Instead, there was an open fire in a hearth. Food was cooked in large iron pots called **cauldrons** which were hung over the fire. For feasts and special occasions, a whole animal such as a pig, ox, or even a deer, would be skinned and put on to a spit. The meat was then turned round and round over the fire so that it cooked evenly and did not burn.

At table in richer houses, *trenchers* were being replaced by plates made of **pewter**, silver, or pottery. These were better for holding the sauces and gravies which went with many dishes. For years, people had eaten with their fingers, cutting meat with a knife, and scooping up broth with a spoon. The first forks had two prongs (or **tines**), and were used to serve food rather than to eat with it.

Some of the townspeople would eat and drink heavily at a feast to make up for weeks of a boring diet, consisting of broth, rye and barley bread, with ale. There would be music, dancing, **bull-baiting** and bear-baiting, and cock-fights. At the end of the feast, some people would have 'guzzled, and become cupshotten (drunk)'.

In 1600 a French writer called Thomas Artus made fun of diners who were having difficulties using a fork for the first time. (At this time, people were not allowed even to touch the food with their hands.)

'. . . They took it [the salad] with their forks . . . then they were served some artichokes, asparagus, peas, and shelled broad beans, and it was a delight to see them eating all this with their forks. For those who were not as nimble-fingered as the others, they dropped as much on their plates, the dishes, and all around, as they put in their mouths. . . .'

◁ A wooden engraving by Arcimboldo of kitchen equipment. Like the fruit and vegetables on page 5, they have been put together to look like a very odd man: a fork, bellows, and a **mortar** are among the items.

▽ This 16th century picture shows a kitchen scene. The cook holds a skimmer in his left hand. This was used to skim off fat or unwanted pieces of food from the top of a cauldron. He is also holding a spoon and tasting the food.

Families ate together, and they all ate the same food. Children and women ate less than men, we are told, but everyone drank ale or watered-down wine. It was not safe to drink milk or water. Meat was banned on Fridays, and during Lent (the forty days before Easter), when fish was served.

It is hard for us to imagine that the only way of making fresh food last was to cure it with salt or smoke. There was no **refrigeration**, although ice houses were built in big houses so that guests could add ice to their drinks. Food went bad very quickly, and strong sauces and spices were used to cover up the awful tastes and smells.

Diet and health

Manners for children

(rules from a book made in 1577)

'Scratche not thy head with thy fingers when thou arte at thy meate; Picke not thy teeth with thy knife nor with thy fingers ende;

Fyll not thy mouth too full, lest thou perhaps must speak; Nor blow out thy crums when thou dost eate.

Foule not the place with spitting where thou dost sit.'

◁ This engraving is 'January' from *The Twelve Months* made by Etienne Delaune in 1568. It shows diners being served in a separate room, while the cook works at an open fire in the kitchen. Wine is being poured, and you can see a *trencher* on the table. The dogs wait patiently for scraps of food.

No one knew much about which foods were good or bad for you. In summer, fruit would sometimes over-ripen in the heat. Anyone who ate it had **diarrhoea**, so people thought the fruit itself was the cause and could be bad for you.

People ate a lot of sweet things. This rotted their teeth and turned them black. Paintings of the time rarely show us this, but when Henry VII died in 1509, a description of him at the time read: '. . . small blue eyes, only a few

▷ In this woodcut made by Hans Burgkmair in 1542, a cook is grilling fish and tasting the sauces that will go with it.

Shakespeare's play, *King Henry IV*, Part II, is about life in the time of King Henry IV (1399 to 1413). However, Shakespeare is really painting a picture of life at the time he wrote the play, which was first performed in 1597 or 1598. Master Shallow describes the food he would like William the cook to prepare for him:

'. . . Some pigeons . . . a couple of short-legged hens, a joint of mutton and any pretty little tiny kickshaws. . .'

'Kickshaws' (from the French *quelques choses*, which means 'some things') were small **delicacies**.

blackish teeth, thin white hair, and a pale face.'

People in the 16th century thought that their health was governed by four 'humours'. They also believed that these four emotional states were affected by what they ate. So, depending on whether they were 'sanguine' (steady), 'phlegmatic' (calm and quiet), 'choleric' (short-tempered and angry), or 'melancholic' (sad and depressed), they needed to eat different kinds of foods – dry or moist, hot or cold.

Pasta made from flour and elaborate sugar **confectionery** were new foods, while olives and grapes became more common. Gradually, people began to realise that simple food, fresh vegetables in salads, eggs and fruit, were what people needed to stay well.

We have a good idea of what food was available in English cities at this time. French nobles, fleeing from the dangers of the Wars of Religion between Catholics and **Protestants** in France, were provided with a phrase book. This described the types of food and the dishes they would be likely to find on arrival in England. But the picture of town and city life that we see most clearly shows filth, poverty and disease.

▽ In this market, there is a rich selection of fruits, including cherries and grapes. The woman has artichokes in her basket. The men are perhaps travellers who have arrived in the city and are having a glass of wine while the women do the shopping.

Dishes served to French Huguenots

The Huguenots were French people who did not follow the teachings of the Catholic Church. They were Protestants.

- leg of mutton with garlick
- venison pastie with sugared mustard
- capon (chicken) and leeks
- blackbirds, larks and partridges
- pike and carp
- hare and veal, as rare delicacies
- roasted apples and pears
- 'scrapped' [small pieces of] cheese

Food for nobles and royals

In the sixteenth century, life at court became grander and the feasts were more extravagant. Although this was a way of living that only a tiny part of the population enjoyed, we have many records from the time – paintings, journals and diaries from visitors, and account books. The English royal court consisted of 1200 courtiers in winter and about 800 in summer. (Many courtiers visited their homes, away from London, in the summer months.) This was a great many mouths to feed.

A royal kitchen

△ A fete at Bermondsey, London, which was then in leafy countryside. Dancers, musicians and the honoured guests (far right) stand before a feast about to be served.

Many of the Tudor royal palaces still stand, and some have been restored to show the kitchens and dining halls as they must have been at the time. Hampton Court, near London, was the home of Cardinal Wolsey until 1529, and then of his king, Henry VIII. Its Tudor kitchens are the largest and most complete in Europe.

◁ The people who ran the kitchens and dining halls at Hampton Court were known as the Board of the Greencloth. The Latin words – *ratio* (reason), *intellectus* (intelligence), *discretio* (discretion) – are all ways of encouraging the Board to do its job well.

Rooms in the kitchens at Hampton Court

spicery	to store spices
chaundry	to store candles
flesh larder	where fresh meat such as deer or wild boar was kept
wet larder	where fish was kept fresh and cool in seaweed
bakery	where bread was made and baked
boiling house	held the cauldron for boiling and softening meat

The kitchen area at Hampton Court was built in 1514, and added to by Henry VIII. In it, three master cooks worked, helped by twelve assistants, and seven *gallopynes*, boys whose job it was to turn the spit. The boys were given ale to quench their thirst.

In the boiling house there was a large cauldron in which meat was boiled to soften it before making broth. It held about 250 litres. The bakery was built near the river's edge in case of fire. Fresh water was piped in from springs in Kingston, about 8 kilometres away. Rubbish, of course, went straight into the river.

Fine feasts

Royal feasts consisted of many dishes, but they were usually served as two courses. However, these courses were not like the single dishes at meals today. Instead, they were more like a **buffet** with a wide choice of dishes, both savoury and sweet. Some were served in a *messe* (a dish for two or four people). This saved time as the servants rushed to and fro, trying to attend to everyone.

A Spanish nobleman visiting Hampton Court for the first time describes the scene: 'There are 18 kitchens going at full blast. They seem a veritable hell such is the stir and bustle in them.'

At the feast of St John's Day, Midsummer's Day, 24 June 1542, we know that the following 'menu' was served:

First course
Cheat and *manchet* bread
Beer and ale
Wine
Chines of beef with vinegar sauce
Pestells [pies] of red deer
Baked carp in wine with prunes
Butter and eggs
Wafers

Second course
Boiled mutton
Swan
Cocks
Roast boar with pudding
Cream of almonds
Wafers
Marchpanes [Marzipan]

An Elizabethan feast in 1588
The food served included: 'joints of venison roasted in rye, sides of beef, boars' heads; bacon, calves' feet, ham, game pies with cinnamon; peacock, herons, blackbirds, larks; salmon, eels, turbot, whiting, sprats, oysters; sweetmeats, syrups, jellies, candied roses and violets, grapes, oranges, almonds, hazel nuts; cakes and sugar-soaked confections.'

Food was often served in two sittings at feasts in order to fit in all the people. The king himself rarely attended these feasts. He had his own rooms in which food was served that had been cooked specially for him. Even when Queen Elizabeth attended a royal feast in 1588, she had someone to taste all her food before she ate it, in case an enemy had poisoned it.

Some of the dishes which were served at feasts in palaces were very **elaborate**. Swans and peacocks were cooked whole, and their beaks decorated with gold paint. There were also sugar shapes, sometimes spun like thread. These were known as **subtleties**, and were often made with *marchpane* (marzipan).

Vast quantities of ale and wine were drunk at feasts. At Hampton Court, 300 barrels of beer were consumed each year. Wine and port from France, Spain and Portugal were kept in cellars below the kitchens.

Royal shows

This was also a time of great competition between nations, especially old enemies such as France and Spain. Each wanted to outdo the other in terms of grandeur and the display of wealth. In 1520, Henry VIII and François I put

▽ This extravagant scene shows the Field of the Cloth of Gold outside Calais in 1520. On the far right, food is being served in a tent.

△ This Italian woodcut shows the main kitchen (*cucina principale*) in a big house. Note the plates on the table, the knives on the wall, and the joint of meat being roasted on the spit.

Henry VII went on what he called a royal progress. He paid for some of his food – a shilling [5p] for beer, one shilling and eightpence [8p] for cherries and strawberries, and three shillings and fourpence [17p] for corn in someone's field (which his deer ate by mistake)!

on a great show outside Calais. This was a form of royal showing off, known as the Field of the Cloth of Gold. Paintings of the event show an open air feast being served in tents. Fortunately, it seems, the weather was good.

Guests at the French banquet, or *masquerade*, at Bayonne in 1565 were not so lucky. A pavilion was built on an island in the river. Horses were disguised as elephants, and boats were decorated to look like whales. Soldiers wore costumes to make them look like shepherdesses.

Unfortunately, a thunderstorm broke in the middle of the banquet. Rain poured down. The 'whales' ran on to the banks, and the royal guests were drenched. However, the tapestry of the event made for the royal family shows the scene appearing to take place under a clear blue sky.

Royal travels

Tudor kings and queens moved around to meet their people. Travelling was difficult, so this could be done only in the summer.

Elizabeth I often ended her summer travels at Charlecote Park near Warwick. Here, open-air feasts and celebrations including firework displays and concerts took place.

In 1564 Catherine de Medici and her nine-year-old son, Charles IX, set off on a journey round France that lasted two years. A master cook and five assistants went with them. Local people who helped probably learned new ways of cooking from them.

▽ A royal picnic, perhaps at Charlecote Park. Queen Elizabeth I is being waited on, while members of her court sit on the ground and enjoy the food and drink.

Food for travellers

William Harrison wrote about the inns of England in glowing terms. Certainly, they were admired by visitors from other countries. 'In all our inns we have plenty of ale, beer, and sundry kinds of wine, and such is the capacity of them that they are able to lodge two or three hundred persons and their horses at ease, and with very short warning, make such provision for their diet that may seem incredible to any-one not acquainted with them.'

Travel over land in Europe in Tudor times was slow and difficult. A message could be sent from Edinburgh to London in three days, but only by using horses and changing them every 16 kilometres or so at **post-houses**. No good roads had been built since Roman times, more than 1,000 years earlier. In winter, rain caused floods and mud, while snow and ice could slow progress even more. Local people sometimes cut down trees or bushes blocking a road, or filled in the biggest holes. Highway robbers and **footpads** were a real danger.

Many rivers were no longer **navigable**, having silted up over the years. Only the estuaries that were also ports, such as Bristol and London, could take ships. It was quicker to send corn or wool from Wales by sea. Coal from Newcastle also reached London more quickly by sea than by land.

We are used to fresh food arriving quickly from all over the world, but in Tudor times food had to be grown and provided where it was needed. No one knew that keeping food frozen made it last longer. Salting, curing and pickling were the common ways of preserving

▽ The cooks prepare the food for travellers at an inn while a guest waits patiently. The man on the left is probably the innkeeper. He may be carrying a lamp.

A phrase book used by French people travelling in England at the time advised the traveller to ask the chambermaid: 'My she friend, is my bed made? Is it good? Pull off my hose [stockings], and warm my bed . . .I thank you, fair maiden.'

▽ This Italian open air kitchen shows all the equipment a travelling cook would need – cauldrons, spits and cooking pots, as well as bowls and plates. The food was roasted on a spit, or boiled.

food. For the traveller, food was a problem. It led to the setting up of inns and taverns on the main routes. Here travellers could change or feed their horses, eat a good meal and spend a dry, warm night before continuing their journey. Many of these inns still stand, and provide some of the same **hospitality**.

In spite of the difficulties, in Europe, people began to travel more. This affected what they knew or could learn from other countries. Italy was now at the heart of learning and religion, the Holy Roman Empire. Catherine de Medici, the Florentine bride of Henri II, came to France from Italy in the late 1590s. She (and others) brought changes to people's choice of food, and to the way in which it was served.

Explorers and traders

While land travel was much the same as it had been for hundreds of years, there was a huge increase in sea travel during the 16th century. The main reason for this was the search for new trading routes, and greater riches. The Spanish conquered Mexico and large parts of

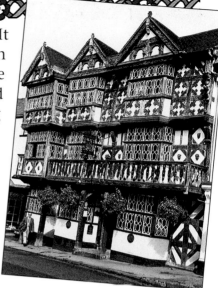

△ A Dutch merchant, visiting The Feathers Inn at Ludlow, in England, wrote: 'The neat cleanliness, the pleasant and delightful furniture in every point for the household, wonderfully rejoiced me.'

A student's diary

A Swiss medical student, Felix Platter, travelled from Basel to Montpellier to study. His diary tells us about food and travel. Before he left home, Platter's mother cooked him a quail he had kept as a pet for his last supper. On his journeys he was constantly at risk from cheats, robbers and bad food. At one inn he was even served with a pie made from cat meat.

In France Platter lodged with a family who did not eat pork. Mutton was the usual meat, with plenty of cabbage and root vegetables. Platter got into trouble for eating eggs during Lent, which was forbidden. He tried olives, noted the arrival of cherries in spring, the onion fair at the end of August, and the wine harvest. After receiving his degree, he and fellow students paraded through the town carrying fennel stalks coated in sugar. To celebrate, they drank mulled wine made with herbs, called *hypocras*.

▷ 'The Amerindian town of Secoton in 1580,' by John White. Secoton was in what is now Virginia, USA. The maize (corn) on the right is, from the top, 'rype [ripe]', 'green' and 'newly sprong [sprung]'.

the Caribbean and South America, returning with gold, silver and precious stones. Exploration led to settlement, or **colonisation**. Ships returning to Europe with treasure were often attacked, and their precious cargo stolen.

The voyagers brought back new foods from their travels. Herbs and spices which could not be grown in the colder European climate started to appear: ginger, nutmeg, peppers – and sugar. Potatoes are said to have come from North America, as well as tomatoes. Sailors from Venice went to Mexico and exchanged grain for sugar cane. They brought back turkeys for the first time. Maize (or corn) was a new vegetable, although historians believe maize may have been grown in China and the Middle East.

Sailors who travelled on voyages of exploration, or stole treasure from ships on the high seas, had to spend many months away from land in terrible conditions. There was no fresh water. The ale and wine would go sour, and the hard ship's biscuit would become full of

At the time of the explorers' arrival in America, a Navajo medicine man was recorded as saying: 'Joy and beauty, may the sweet yellow maize accompany you to the end of the earth.'

maggots. The dried meat and fish was so tough that it had to be boiled for a long time to soften it up. In the process it lost most of its flavour. No one at the time understood the value of fresh fruit and vegetables, and many sailors died of **scurvy** and other diseases.

Writing about food

Many writers at the time complained about the huge amount of food eaten at banquets. They said that people would be harmed by mixing dishes, and by eating too many rich sauces.

A French writer, François Rabelais, wrote of an imaginary country ruled by a demanding king known as 'Sir Belly'. The people of this country were called 'gastrolators', and they had to please Sir Belly by offering him food all the time. Rabelais' story of 'Sir Belly' was in fact about France, and the way people's eating habits were changing. These changes which started in Tudor times were to continue throughout Europe for both rich and poor people over the next couple of centuries.

▽ 'An old woman cooking eggs', by the Spanish painter Velazquez (1599-1660). The food is being cooked over a charcoal stove.

▽ This 16th century feast has not been made to look more elegant than it really was! People are eating with their fingers, and drinking out of mugs, while dogs sniff round the floor for bones and bits of meat.

Meals and recipes

Dinner at Sulgrave Manor, 1572

Venison pie with sugared mustard
roast shoulder of veal
roast leg of mutton stuffed with garlic, bread and
cabbage

trout, pickerels (young pike) and salted herrings

capon (chicken) boiled with leeks
pieces of roasted turkey-cock (turkey)
roast partridge

jelly, with candied flowers, gilliflowers (cloves)
and sugar paste

Sulgrave Manor was the Elizabethan home of the ancestors of George Washington, who became the first President of the USA in 1789. Life there was not as grand as in the royal palaces, or in a big house like Charlecote Park. But the family ate well, and the dishes served on special occasions such as the one above, sound delicious. This dinner would have lasted for about three hours, with intervals in which the village fiddler played music for the family and guests.

Children and adults ate together. The father would first bless the food, and during the meal, a toast in watered wine would be made to the monarch, the country and the Washington family. At the end of the meal, a nursemaid would put the children to bed.

New foods

Explorers and travellers brought back many 'new' foods to Europe during Tudor times. Today these foods are enjoyed all over the world. Trucks, trains and planes can transport fresh produce quickly from one part of the world to another.

Tudor cooks relied on fresh food that was produced locally. They used more preserved foods in winter when there was less fresh produce available. Food which is preserved by drying, salting or pickling tastes different from preserved food today – which is usually canned or frozen. The meals you make will not taste the same as the ones served at Sulgrave Manor in Tudor times.

> **WARNING:** Sharp knives and boiling liquids are dangerous. Hot ovens and pans can burn you. *Always ask an adult to help you* when you are preparing or cooking food in the kitchen.

Pain Perdue – French Toast

Pain perdue means 'lost bread' in French. This is a recipe to use up stale or leftover bread which would otherwise have been thrown away or 'lost'. Today we call this dish French toast.

Ingredients

4 large slices of wholemeal *or* white bread

3 eggs

a pinch of salt

1/2 tsp cinnamon

25 g (1 oz) butter

30 ml (2 tbs) cooking oil

2 tsp caster sugar

Ask an adult to help you when you start to cook.

1. Slice the bread and cut off the crusts. Take care to keep your fingers away from the blade of the knife.
2. Break the eggs into a small mixing bowl. Add the salt and cinnamon and whisk the mixture well.
3. Weigh out the butter and put it in the frying pan. Measure out the oil and add it to the butter in the pan.
4. Pour the beaten egg mixture into a shallow dish.
5. Place the frying pan over a very low heat so that the butter melts. Stir the melted butter and oil together. Take care that the mixture does not burn.
6. Quickly dip the slices of bread in and out of the egg mixture. Make sure that both sides of each slice of bread are well covered with the egg mixture.
7. Transfer the bread to the frying pan and fry until golden brown on both sides.
8. Put the bread onto a serving dish *or* plates and sprinkle caster sugar over each slice.

Equipment

bread knife

bread board

small mixing bowl

whisk

scales

shallow dish

frying pan

spatula

serving dish *or* plates

teaspoon

Sharp knives, hot liquids and pans are dangerous.

Chicken Blancmange

In Tudor times this light and tasty dish was served to people who were not well. A recipe for this dish was first printed in a 16th century French cookery book.

Ingredients

1 chicken stock cube

300 ml (¹/₂ pint) water

450 g (1 lb) chicken breast fillets

¹/₄ tsp ground cardamom

¹/₂ tsp ground ginger

1 drop of almond essence

6–8 blanched almonds

15 ml (1 tsp) caster sugar

1. Measure out the water and pour it into a large saucepan. Bring the water to the boil and add the chicken stock cube. Stir the water until the stock cube has dissolved.
2. Ask an adult to take the skin off the chicken breasts for you. Then put the meat into the saucepan with the chicken stock.
3. Turn the heat down, so that the stock boils gently. Let the meat cook in the stock for about 30 minutes. Ask an adult to test the meat to make sure it is cooked.
4. Take the saucepan off the heat and allow the stock and meat to cool, for about 20 minutes. Use a slotted spoon to take the meat out of the saucepan.
5. Ask an adult to put the meat through a food processor *or* meat mincer for you, so that the meat is finely ground into a stiff paste.
6. Put the meat into a mixing bowl and add the cardamom, ginger and almond essence. Mix everything together well with a fork. Gradually add about 3 tbs of the chicken stock from the saucepan. The mixture should be stiff but not dry.
7. Spoon the mixture into a serving dish and smooth it down with the back of the spoon. Decorate the dish with almonds and sprinkle a little caster sugar over the top.
8. If you are not going to eat the dish immediately, put it in the refrigerator and serve it chilled.

Equipment

measuring jug

large saucepan

wooden spoon

slotted spoon

food processor *or* meat mincer

large mixing bowl

fork

serving dish

Sharp knives, hot liquids and pans are dangerous.

Broad beans and bacon

1. Put the broad beans in a large saucepan and cover them with cold water. Bring the water to the boil and then turn the heat down. Cook the beans for about 10 minutes, until they are tender.
2. When the beans are cooked take the saucepan off the heat. Strain the beans and leave them in the colander to cool.
3. Carefully chop the parsley very fine, taking care to keep your fingers away from the knife blade.

Ingredients

450 g (1 lb) shelled fresh *or* frozen broad beans

water

30 ml (2 tbs) freshly chopped parsley

50 g (2 oz) streaky bacon

15 g (¹/₂ oz) butter

¹/₄ tsp salt

¹/₄ tsp black pepper

Ask an adult to help you when you start to cook.

Equipment

large saucepan

colander

sharp knife

chopping board

scales

large frying pan

spatula *or* wooden spoon

serving dish

Sharp knives, hot liquids and pans are dangerous.

4. Carefully cut the bacon into small pieces, with a sharp knife. Then weigh out the butter and cut it into small pieces.

5. Put the butter in the frying pan and let it melt over a low heat. Then stir in the bacon pieces and turn up the heat a little.

6. When the bacon is almost cooked, add the broad beans, chopped parsley, black pepper and salt.

7. Stir the mixture well so that the beans are covered in bacon and parsley. Then remove the frying pan from the heat.

8. Put the mixture in a dish and serve immediately.

Roast apples

In Tudor times these would have been roasted on a spit, in the same way as a turkey or a chicken. In this recipe the apples are 'roasted' in the oven and could be served with roast pork or after roast turkey or a chicken.

1. Ask an adult to set the oven to 200°C (400°F).

2. Wash the apples and dry them. Ask an adult to core the apples for you and to make a slit in the skin with a sharp knife all the way round the centre of each apple.

3. Put the sugar, cinnamon, dates and raisins in a mixing bowl and stir them well, until the fruit is well covered in sugar and cinnamon.

4. Stick a clove inside the top and the bottom of the hole which goes through the middle of each apple. Then stand the apples in the roasting tin.

5. Carefully stuff each apple with the two dates and four raisins. Then fill up the hole in each apple with the sugar and cinnamon mixture.

6. Pour a tablespoon of water over the top of each apple so that there is a little water underneath each one.

7. Ask an adult to put the roasting tin into the oven for you. Let the apples cook for about 40 to 50 minutes.

8. Ask an adult to take the tin out of the oven for you and to put the apples on a serving dish. They can be eaten hot or cold.

Ingredients

4 large cooking apples

4 tbs dark brown sugar

30 ml (2 tsp) ground cinnamon

8 large stoned dates

14 large stoned raisins

8 cloves

60 ml (4 tbs) water

Equipment

apple corer

sharp knife

mixing bowl

spoon

roasting tin

serving dish

Ask an adult to help you when you start to cook.

Glossary

ale: An alcoholic drink, like beer, usually made from hops, malt, water and yeast. In Tudor times ale was made without hops.

banquet: A grand feast or public dinner.

brine: Salty water. Food stored in brine will keep in good condition.

broadcasting: Scattering over a large area.

broth: A thin mixture of vegetables and water, drunk hot like a soup.

buffet: A meal laid out on a table from which guests served themselves.

bull-baiting: The sport of setting dogs to tease or excite a bull.

cauldron: A large pot, usually made of iron, for cooking over an open fire.

colonisation: Rule by a government over another (or part of another) country.

confectionery: Sweets or pastries.

delicacy: A very small but tasty portion of food, which could be eaten in one mouthful.

diarrhoea: A stomach upset which results in frequent and mainly liquid bowel movements to get rid of the waste matter.

dynasty: A series of rulers who are members of the same family, or the period of time during which members of the same family rule.

elaborate: Put together very carefully, and often with many different parts.

enclosed: Surrounded or fenced off.

famine: A time when people starve because there is not enough food.

feudal: Describes the way in which people held and worked the land for landowners during the Middle Ages. The feudal system slowly changed in Tudor times.

footpad: A highway robber who travelled on foot rather than on horse-back.

game: Animals, birds and fish which are hunted for food and for sport.

harrow: A frame with spikes attached to it, that is pulled over the ground to break up the earth.

hospitality: A friendly welcome given to visitors or guests, which usually includes the offer of meals and drinks.

import: Goods brought into one country from another.

manor: The area of land and property given to a noble by the ruler.

merchant: A person who bought and sold goods, often from other countries.

monarch: A ruler of a country – for example, a king, queen or emperor.

mortar: A strong bowl or dish in which foods were ground into small pieces or powder, using a club or stick called a pestle.

navigable: Describes a stretch of water along which boats can be sailed or steered.

offal:	The parts of an animal cut out during butchering, such as kidneys, heart, lungs, stomach or liver.
pewter:	A metal made from a mixture of tin and lead, which was often used in Tudor times to make mugs, plates and serving dishes.
post-house:	A house where horses were kept for travellers. Travelling a long distance and changing horses regularly was called posting.
pottage:	A soup or stew, thickened with vegetables, pulses or grains until it was almost solid, like porridge.
preserve:	To treat food or drink so that it would keep for a long time without going bad.
Protestants:	People who belonged to one of the Christian churches that separated from the Church of Rome in the 16th century.
refrigeration:	The process of making, or keeping, something cold, usually to preserve it.
Renaissance:	This word means rebirth in French. It is the name used to describe the period in Europe from the 14th to the 16th centuries, when there was a revival (rebirth) of interest in the arts and learning. It was based on studies of ancient civilisations, particularly those of the ancient Greeks and Romans.
scurvy:	A skin disease which people suffer from if they don't eat enough food which contains Vitamin C. This vitamin occurs mainly in fresh fruit and vegetables.
sewage:	Mainly liquid waste matter that is carried away from buildings through pipes, channels or ditches.
spit:	A long thin metal bar, often pointed at one end, on which food is fixed to be cooked.
stocks:	A heavy wooden framework made with holes and fastenings for the feet and arms. People were held in the stocks as a punishment. The stocks were in public places, such as the village square, so that everyone could see who was being punished.
subtleties:	Delicate, and often highly decorated, food made mostly with sugar.
tavern:	A place where ale, beer and wine was sold and drunk. Taverns often served hot meals as well.
threshing:	Separating grain from its stalk.
tines:	The prongs, teeth or points of a fork or comb.

Further reading

Country Life, Tony Triggs, 'Tudors & Stuarts' series (Wayland Publishers Limited, 1993)

Elizabethan Life, Stewart Ross, 'How it Was' series (B.T.Batsford, 1991)

Exploration by Sea, Struan Reid, 'The Silk and Spice Routes' series (Belitha Press, 1993)

Food, Peter Chrisp, 'Tudors & Stuarts' series (Wayland Publishers Limited, 1994)

Pot Luck – Cooking and Recipes from the Past, Jo Lawrie (A & C Black, 1991)

Tudor Towns, Joanne Jessop, 'Beginning History' series (Wayland Publishers Limited, 1990)

Index